MATH IN OUR WORLD

USING MATH
TO MAKE PARTY PLANS

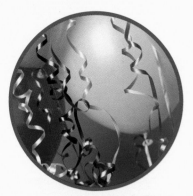

By Joan Freese
Photographs by Gregg Andersen

Reading consultant: Susan Nations, M.Ed.,
author/literacy coach/consultant in literacy development
Math consultant: Rhea Stewart, M.A., mathematics content specialist

WEEKLY READER®
PUBLISHING

Please visit our web site at www.garethstevens.com
For a free color catalog describing our list of high-quality books,
call 1-800-542-2595 (USA) or 1-800-387-3178 (Canada). Our fax: 1-877-542-2596

Library of Congress Cataloging-in-Publication Data

Freese, Joan.
     Using math to make party plans / Joan Freese.
          p. cm. — (Math in our world. Level 2)
       ISBN-13: 978-0-8368-9003-7 (lib. bdg.)
       ISBN-10: 0-8368-9003-5 (lib. bdg.)
       ISBN-13: 978-0-8368-9012-9 (softcover)
       ISBN-10: 0-8368-9012-4 (softcover)
     1. Arithmetic—Juvenile literature. I. Title.
     QA115.F744   2008
     513.2'11—dc22   2007029087

This edition first published in 2008 by
Weekly Reader® Books
An Imprint of Gareth Stevens Publishing
1 Reader's Digest Road
Pleasantville, NY 10570-7000 USA

Senior Editor: Brian Fitzgerald
Creative Director: Lisa Donovan
Graphic Designer: Alexandria Davis

Photo credits: cover & title page Jupiter Images; all other photographs by Gregg Andersen

Printed in the United States of America

1 2 3 4 5 6 7 8 9 10 09 08 07

TABLE OF CONTENTS

Chapter 1: Party Prep 4

Chapter 2: Time to Get Busy 8

Chapter 3: More Work to Do 12

Chapter 4: Party Time! 16

Glossary 24

Words that appear in the glossary are printed in **boldface** type the first time they occur in the text.

Chapter 1:
Party Prep

Mr. Kent's class is having a party. They will mark the 100th day of school. Everyone will help plan! The class will decide what to do at the party. They will decide what food to eat, too.

Children will bring things for the party.
Teams can use math to help them plan.
If they plan well, they will bring just the
right amount of things.

5

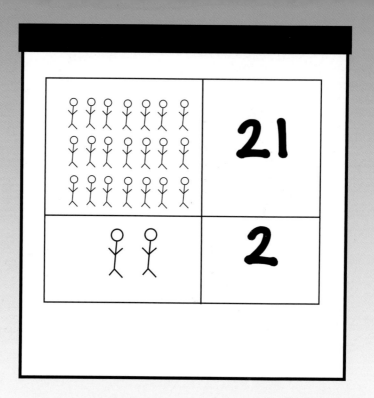

How many people will be at the party? There are 21 children. There will be 2 adults. Mr. Kent will be at the party. There will also be a special guest.

The class writes a **number sentence.** They **add.**

21 + 2 = 23

The **sum** is the number of people who will be at the party.

There will be 23 people in all. The class needs to bring enough food for 23 people. They need to bring enough drinks for everyone, too.

Chapter 2:
Time to Get Busy

Team One will bring muffins. Cindy will bring 12 muffins. Molly will bring some, too. She will bring 14 muffins. How many muffins will they bring in all?

They add to find the answer.

$12 + 14 = 26$

They will have 26 muffins for the party.
What kind of muffins should they bring?
Cindy likes oat muffins. Molly likes
blueberry muffins.

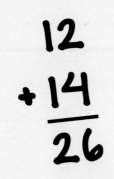

$$\begin{array}{r} 12 \\ + 14 \\ \hline 26 \end{array}$$

Team Two will bring boxes of juice. Chase has a pack that had 36 boxes. The pack is open now. His family drank 11 boxes. They were thirsty! How many boxes are left?

10

Team Two **subtracts** to find the answer.

$36 - 11 = 25$

There are 25 boxes of juice left. That should be enough juice. The pack has many kinds of juice. Everyone will find juice they like to drink.

Chapter 3:
More Work to Do

Team Three will bring balloons. Jordan has 24 blue balloons. Seth has 17 orange ones. Jordan's balloons are left over from a picnic. His dad saved them in a box. Now Jordan can use them for the party.

How many balloons do they have in all?
They add.

24 + 17 = 41

They will have 41 balloons. Seth's mom will
help them blow up the balloons. His mom will
bring them to the party. She cannot stay for
the party, though. She has to go to work.

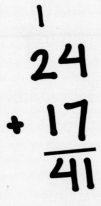

$$\begin{array}{r} \overset{1}{2}4 \\ +\ 17 \\ \hline 41 \end{array}$$

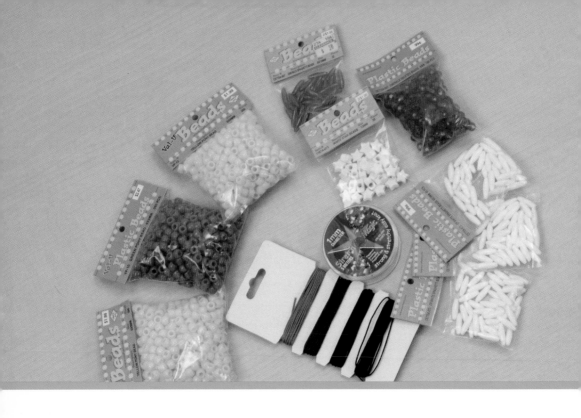

The children will string beads at the party.
Their art teacher has cord they can use.
Team Four has 9 packs of long beads. They
have 21 packs of round beads. How many
more packs of round beads than long beads
do they have?

14

They subtract to find the answer.

21 − 9 = 12

They have 12 more packs of round beads than long beads. The class has plenty of beads in all to use at the party.

$$
\begin{array}{r}
{}^{1}\,{}^{11} \\
2\!\!\!/\,1\!\!\!/ \\
-\ \ 9 \\
\hline
12
\end{array}
$$

Chapter 4:
Party Time!

Today is the 100th day of school. Time for party fun! The principal is here. Her name is Ms. Brown. Welcome, Ms. Brown! She is the special guest.

16

Each child counts 100 beads. The children
string the beads. They make things to wear.
Some children will give their beads to friends.

Mr. Kent has a question. There are five teams. Four teams have done a job for the class party. How many teams have not done a job yet?

That is easy! The children do the math in their heads. Four teams have done jobs. One team has not done a job. That team is ready to work now.

Team Five is excited. They listen to Mr. Kent.
What is their job? He tells them it is an important
job. It is also fun to do.

They will help serve juice and muffins. Let's go, Team Five! Everyone is hungry! The class eats muffins. They drink juice. Some children talk about their beads. They show Ms. Brown what they made.

It is time to clean up. The children throw away the trash. They wipe the tables clean. Good work!

The children had fun stringing beads. They liked their snacks and juice. Everyone had a great time. The class cannot wait to use math to plan another party!

Glossary

add: to join 2 or more numbers

number sentence: 21 + 2 = 23 is a number sentence. 36 − 11 = 25 is also a number sentence.

subtract: to take away one number from another

sum: the number you get from adding numbers together

About the Author

Joan Freese has written extensively for children on nonfiction topics from hip-hop dance to hands-on science projects. She lives with her family in Minneapolis, Minnesota.